Reflections of the Vale

Poems and prose of the Vale of Evesham countryside and beyond

Bob Woodroofe

Greenwood Press

First published in 1997

This impression 2019

Greenwood Press
38 Birch Avenue
Evesham
Worcs. WR11 1YJ

Tel 01386 446477

http://greenwoodpress.co.uk

ISBN 978-0-9521165-1-6

Introduction

'A journey through a year, a life, an area.
As seen through my window on the world.'

This is a further collection of verses about local places, people
and events in the Vale of Evesham and further afield.
They have triggered these responses,
some immediate, some years later.

The wonders of Nature continue to inspire me as well as
John Clare, the Northamptonshire poet and Richard
Jefferies, the Wiltshire writer. May I never tire of them.
I hope that they and I can bring you a brief respite from
today's mad world and some pleasure also.

Bob Woodroofe 1997

Contents

Window

What do you see from your window?
Your picture of the world. Each is different,
a framed collection, based on
clarity of vision, lucidity of dreams,
Carved from our upbringing, surroundings,
family, friends, coloured by life's experience.
Rose tinted by love, misted over by time,
stained by death's pain.
The perspective from our vantage point.
Our own individual panorama.
Hand crafted, each pane lovingly composed
from the fragments of our lives.
Slivers of glass that right through life pass.
Held in place, but putty pliable,
hand moulded imprints, mirrored
in the skylights of your mind.
Looking out into hope's landscape
through the openings of opportunity.
How many times have you balanced on the sill,
longing to venture over the ledge,
held only by the cord linked to your
life's small wheel slowly turning.
Reflections, caught thoughts, locked in the brain
flicker with subconscious imagery over each sepia pane.
Mostly open, sometimes curtained, even closed.
Composed of the past, present, future even.
Take down the shutters, throw back the curtain.
What can you see through your window?

New Year

The snow falls, pure, white, clean, to greet another new year.
The Mistle in the Yew guards his ever ripening berries.
I sit, watching, listen to haunting Celtic music playing.
I dream of that mystic green island, distant family,
ancient links. I will, I must, visit you one day.

I wonder what this new year will bring,
I wish I had more time, precious time.
To do all the things I should, the things I want.

The snow is ever changing, like life,
first falling in small flakes straight down,
then suddenly whirling, dropping thicker and heavier,
pouring down to form a white carpet
over the bright green grass of life.
Life that is forever growing, like the grass.

The Dunnock flits onto the bird table,
picking hungrily at the Christmas crumbs,
sits under its snow decked roof,
sheltering from the falling white flakes.

A new grandchild before Christmas,
another to add to the growing flock,
mother and baby boy doing fine.
The wonder of existence renewed once more.
What will the world hold for him?
Not long now till the twenty first century.
I hope he will grow up to see and appreciate
the things that have given me such joy.

From his first sunrise to last sunset
the ever changing landscape of life.
Special moments, special places along the way,
those special people that you meet
to share this wonderful life with.
To make it as good as they have made mine.

The falling snow has stopped now
the last few flakes waft lazily in the breeze.
Like the snow the words too stop falling.
That flow from somewhere on high ceases.

A whole new year unfolds before you,
so much opportunity, so much to do.
Choose wisely, work hard, you can, you will, succeed.
Press on with hope, with the optimism of life,
something good will surely come your way.

This is not just another New Year's day!

Dead Man's Ait

You always look so peaceful and calm,
your reed fringed waters full of charm.
What secrets do you hold down deep,
what can be seen whilst others sleep.

Plum trees stark against night sky,
Silver meadows lit by pale moon sliding by.
The river in its banks gently sleeved,
early evening mist over the water wreathed.

Badger snuffing over the fields wends his way,
treading well-worn paths through tall stems of hay.
The owl floats ghostly over the mist, white
feathers, by late beams of sunlight, kissed.

The fox, disturbed by hunger from his lair,
pads slowly down the path, sniffing damp air.
He stops to slake his thirst from your bank,
sending voles rustling through rushes rank.

Pushes his nose through your fringing grass,
sees the moon reflected, as if in glass.
The ripples from his tongue gently spread,
rocking the moon and stars to bed.

Your waters, home to pike and eel,
the quietness broken by angler's winding reel.
The moonlight glitters on wisp of line,
a thread descending deep into ancient time.

Long ago your waters ran red,
fierce battle raged, much blood was shed.
De Montfort on three sides by river bounded,
By Avon and Prince Edward's troops surrounded.

Clash of steel, sword and pike,
the bloodshed, carnage, waste of life.
Flash of arrow piercing deep.
Scream of death disturbs your sleep.

Tramp of mailed boot over bridges span,
the Inn still bears the name at Offenham.
Their ghosts inhabit your tranquil backwater,
mute witness to this ancient slaughter.

Below the quiet streams lapping waves,
sleep in peace in your watery graves.
People will always remember your fate,
resting quietly by Dead Man's Ait.

Clare's Countryside

These flat lands where you once did roam.
The Fens and Dykes you knew as home.
This chequered landscape through which you passed,
now turned to wide expanse of prairie vast.

Once enclosure, of which you so despaired
impounded the land for which you cared.
Those hedges that the fields did once surround
are now all cleared to windswept ground.

Whitened pooty shells mark your dead wood,
limestone legacy to where you stood.
No longer can we hear the songbird choir
from your green and pleasant byre.

Burned by stubble fire, straw smoked,
the lungs of your life slowly choked.
Now nothing remains, only barbed wire,
sharp strands of pain as you expire.

Machines now roam where once was life,
your heart ripped out by mechanical knife.
Doused by sprays of killing intent,
each ear of corn with deadly load bent.

To Dragon and Damsel in Fen and Dyke,
to slow moving Bream and voracious Pike.
This chemical cocktail causes such strife,
unseen it obliterates the struggle for life.

No longer to see the wedge tail of Kite,
gliding over your fields, red in the light.
Hear the mew of Buzzard from on high,
soaring weightless through the sky.

Hear all around the joyful sound,
through all your seasons that abound.
The song of Birds, the hum of Bee,
the whisper of wind across the lea.
The busy murmur of warm Summer days,
as children in your meadows played.
The cold moan of the Winter gale,
the hiss of rain, the rattle of hail.

The Bittern booming from the reeds,
the Crossbill extracting Conifer seeds.
The rasp of Corncrake hidden in the grain,
the churr of Nightjar as dusk falls again.

The warble of Nightingale from the wood,
where once you dreamt and quietly stood.
The Wryneck's snakelike slither and hiss,
alas, no more can we see of this.

All this it meant so much to you,
it's plain to see, so clear and true.
I feel the same, of that I'm sure,
it means as much to me, or more.

The wonders that you saw we surely miss.
Dear John, what would you have made of this?
What have we done to this our land,
we must act now, must make a stand

or else it will no longer remain,
only the memory and the pain
will stay with us for ever more
as slowly poisoned to the core,

we stumble on over this our earth,
we must learn that it's true worth
is more to life than you or I,
without our care it all will die.

Market

You stand empty now, desolate, no longer used,
no longer needed, a victim of time, somehow abused.
Thin spindly weeds, struggling for moisture,
push up between the bricks that line your floor.
Bricks that have withstood countless thousands
of boxes, nets, sacks, chips, boots
and hooves sparking on their worn surface.
The iron pens bent and rusty now,
no longer polished smooth by sheep and cow.

Where is the hustle and bustle of market,
the colour, the noise, the hubbub.
Fleets of tractors, vans, lorries that replaced
the handcarts, horses and carts of yesteryear.
Disgorging their loads, hand sown, hand grown,
hand-picked from the surrounding countryside.

Spring greens, rhubarb, asparagus,
summer fruits of strawberry and plum,
autumn's apples, pears and potatoes,
winter cabbages, leeks and sprouts.

The gnarled old market gardeners brown
and weather beaten by the seasons.
Almost a part of the landscape
they blend so intimately into it.

That landscape of small cultivated fields
and orchards each lovingly tended.
Gardens for market that they and their forefathers created
over time by their combined knowledge, labour and sweat.
Gleaning a living from the land,
never comfortable, never secure,
at the mercy of weather, drought, frost.

People pass you now with scarcely a glance,
Standing, waiting, wondering what you will become.
Not what you were, what contribution you made
to the local community, over so many years.

A derelict area, ripe for development,
greedy planners arguing over you,
to see how many houses they can cram on you.
You've stood there all this time witnessed
so much, gradually being worn away by the
Elements. Washed with rain, burnt by sun,
cracked by frost, battered by gales.

Yet you are still there, silent, holding so much
in your fabric, but not knowing how to tell anyone.
Now being slowly dismantled, stripped to your bones,
reclaimed, recycled, for sale to whoever, for whatever.
At least you are being reused, not dead and buried
as hard-core under some road, or in some landfill site.
That would be such an inglorious end to your life.

Your destruction begins as demolition starts,
your life, your history torn apart.
Mortar from between your bricks rudely ripped.
Prising away layers of history tightly gripped.
Stacked on the floor, given a price,
how can they put a value on you, your history.
Lured by big money overseas.
Sacrificed for rich peoples ego's to please.
Will they know from whence you came.
Will they realise, our loss, their gain.

New houses to sit astride your history,
new occupants, unknowing, uncaring.
I passed you by as a boy, a youth, a man.
Never gave a thought the years your history could span.
I see you now so stripped and bare,
at least I remember, I care.

Plas

Such greenery, swathes of it, clothing the hillside.
Ancient Oaks clinging to the rocks.
endless seas of conifers draped over the mountains.
Grey weathered outcrops stand, exposed, too steep to plant.

The river winds below, sinuous, brown.
The wind ruffling its waters forming upstream wavelets
against the flow of water from mountain to sea.

A lone fisherman, clothed in olive, stands on the bend
where the flow scours and deepens the channel
against the far bank, he was not visible until he moved,
the sunlight glinting off his rod and spider thread line.

The fields, dotted with sheep, rest in the valley along the river,
its course followed by flecks of stark white, floating
on the wind, wheeling, diving to seek some morsel below.

Clouds slide overhead trailing shadows over the lush fields.
changing scenes of light and dark, endless shades of green.
Stratus envelops the peaks, disappears into the grey mist
to suddenly re-appear again, bathed in light once more.
It can be seen, experienced, but not captured, it is free.

It would be wonderful except for the traffic, engines straining,
reverberating between the mountains, whining, rumbling.
A continuous cacophony of sound, what an intrusion.
Stereo roads, cars snarling defiantly at each other
across the valley, polluting it with their noise, their fumes.

It should be still, peaceful, you should be able to listen to
the wind sighing in the trees, the bubble of Curlew.
The clamour of Gull, chack of Jackdaw,
croak of Raven, instead of this incessant din.

A lamb calls, bleating, hopelessly
drowned by this sea of road noise.
If only we could shut it off, turn it down,

But how did we get here, the same way, by car.
Only adding to the noise, the intrusion.
What is the answer, is there an answer.
How can we audibly destroy such a place.

Jewelled Wings

I see you sweet butterfly and my heart sings
as you pass me by on jewelled wings.
From flower to flower in freedom's flight,
sipping nectar from morn till night.

Your beauty adorns the fresh Spring scene,
underwing patterned, mottled moss green.
In Ladies smock flowers your eggs to slip,
male's gaudy wings with orange splashed tip.

Brimstone with finely sculptured wing,
flash of sulphur, first sign of Spring.
Tripping along the hedgerow bright,
searching for Buckthorn by sun's watery light.

Camouflaged in woodland glade,
settled on leaf, part sun, part shade.
Speckled Wood, dappled with light,
suddenly, you flicker into life.

Up through hazed beams of light,
in territorial fight or nuptial flight.
Spiralling, tracing circles to such a height,
over treetops disappear from sight.

White Admiral, majestically you glide
on planed wing along the ride.
In Blackberry blossom your tongue to
dip, drink sweet nature, sip by sip.

Small copper, flash of burnished gold,
so dainty, fragile, jewel to behold.
Bright orange metalled hue, just
like molten sun, poured over you.

Skipper, busy, here you skip, here you fly, buzzing
from flower to flower, happily you pass each hour.
Full of life, full of the joys of living,
heedless of the pleasure you're giving.

Comma, white marked on mottled wing of gauze,
nature's own punctuation, as you pause
to bask with tawny wings spread wide,
then glide with ragged edge along the ride.

Subtle chocolate and cream, chequerboard black and white,
Jostling on sky blue Scabious in sun's warmth and light.
In flower decked meadows, fresh and green, surrounded
by a dancing, marbled cloud, as in a dream.

See Chalkhill Blues, stand in wonder to gaze
on steep hillside, alive with your fluttering haze.
As if with the chalk itself dusted, moving,
swaying, with down's breeze gusted.

Each and every year may I see you fly,
across flower decked fields, below blue sky.
Such variety of colour, shape and form,
you bring to us each Summer warm.

Butterfly, memory of summer, sun sparkled wing,
what beauty, what joy to me you bring.
Each time I see you my heart lifts,
You are truly one of nature's finest gifts.

Ancient Track

Across rolling hills, your wide green way wends,
into the landscape you so intimately blend.
From Avebury, to Barbury and on,
past Liddington and Waylands to Uffington.
From stone circle to castle, ancient burial mound,
drinking in your history, the legends that abound.
Past carved horses, chalked white into your flanks,
sweet flowers and butterflies dancing on your banks.
Across hills and valleys, carved by glacier's hand,
glimpse prehistoric fields, marked on the land.
Littered with sarsens that the ice has dropped.
Smoothed boulders in green carpet closely cropped.
Wind freshens and gusts along the dusty track,
see the storm clouds approaching, threatening, black.
Shelter under spreading bough of Beech
where the pearls of rain cannot reach.
Cloud passes, sky lightens, rain ceases.
Sheep bleat, still dry, safe in oily fleeces.
Pale sun gleams, fresh smell of newly watered earth,
what price are simple moments such as these worth.
Spring dew on fresh growth of green.
Golden summer corn with poppies adorn the scene.
Fields all shorn bare, harvest time.
Mists of autumn. Winter fog and rime.
Hazy horizon shimmering, misty in the heat.
The rain against your face coldly beat.
Wind sculpted hedges by gale tossed.
Cloud trails in golden sunset lost.
Lost in time, space, sky, breeze,
you never, ever, fail to please.

Avalon

Mystic isle, rising from Sedgemoor Vale,
legend of Joseph and the Holy Grail.
Glastonbury, Isle of Avalon so dear,
were Arthur and Guinevere buried here.
Ancient thorn, that on Wearyall stands,
did Joseph once hold you in his hands.
Your blossoms at Christmas still to be found
upon the hill and hallowed ground.
Is it fable, is it myth, or more.
Did he land on your swampy shore,
Plant his staff and watch it grow.
Build that first chapel long ago.
St. Michael's tower on your heights
some say on ancient Ley line sights.
Earth's energy, mysteriously arranged in lines,
elemental rods deflect, perceive the signs.
Linking sacred sites, where worship was held,
from whence these unknown forces welled.
As you quietly enter, the ambience enthrals,
peace and tranquillity within your walls.
Chalice well, spring so pure, of Christ bled,
iron reddens your shimmering stream's bed.
Soak up the water's flowing sounds.
Was the Holy Grail hidden in your grounds.
Glastonbury, thoughts of you drive this pen,
why are we drawn to you, time and again.
Such haunting beauty and atmosphere lures,
Avalon, your myth and legend still endures.

Up on the Downs

Up here, on the downs, my worries cease,
my pace slackens, I am at peace.
As if climbing up, the urgency
to get here, has purged me, set me free.

I am at home here, with nature so pure,
so much so that my spirits soar.
Up here, nearer the sky, on the fresh breeze,
under the warm sun, so much at ease.

Vapour trails maze across blue sky.
Distant toy cars rush madly by.
Wonderful to put this crazy world aside.
Rest in grassy coombe under heaven so wide.

Butterflies shoot like stars through daylight hours,
over green sward sky, spattered with planet flowers.
Devil's bit, Thistle, Rampion on the breeze nods,
fuel for Adonis blue, nectar from the gods.

Wind rustling through leaves as you pass
over wheat seas ruffled in waving grass.
Chalk fragment in hand from tropical seas.
Harebells tinkle in south scented breeze.

Resting on sky-lined tumuli, I dream,
mining deep into history's rich seam,
above ancient warrior in chalk coat wrapped,
an island time capsule, by hill sea lapped.

By light and cloud shadows these downs
caressed, your grave is surely, truly, blest.
Visible from afar cross rolling hills,
from vale below, by farmer as he tills.

All this smoothes the frowning, furrowed
brow, harrows level the ridge and plough.
The soft rolling contours of this land,
in peace and beauty, left alone, to stand.

Like the downs in mind's space to hold,
light and air, freedom for the heart and soul.
I know these visions will forever dance across
the mind's eye opened by this airy expanse.

The Orchard
Early Morning, a pale late summer sun gleams,
the Orchard waits, hushed, expectant.
Boughs heavy with fruit, ripe for harvesting.
As you enter, the dew clothing the Rabbit cropped grass
washes your boots, you leave footprints down the rows,
break the glistening cobweb strands linking the grass stems.

The Rabbits scurry to safety in the hedgerow
amongst the tangled mass of briars. The Little Owl,
eyes glaring, floats noiselessly away between the trees.
A Pigeon, in contrast, clatters through the branches,
sending a shower of dew pattering to the ground.

Plums, ice cold to the touch, that splash of dew fresh
pearls of water as you pluck each fruit from the branch.
The dew, evaporated by your body warmth,
steams into the morning air from your hands.
The heat of your fingers turns the hoar frost to water,
breaking the patina, changing the colours
into a multitude of subtle shades and hues,
yellow-greens of Pershore, pink-reds of
Victoria, rich purples of Egg and Damson.

As you ascend your ladder into this leafy world,
the branches envelop you in a green embrace.
Climbing upwards you break through this green intimacy
to survey a different scene from your lofty perch.
Smooth and level, stretching away across the Vale,
the early orange ball of sun bathing it in warmth,
lighting this aerial world of rounded green domes,
quiet and calm above the busy scene below.

The clatter of boxes, the quiet rumble of plums
from basket to box, the steady chug of tractor,
the waft of warm diesel as it passes below,
collecting Nature's harvest to disgorge from your heart,
boxes brimful of sweet plums bound for market.
The voices hulloing down the rows,
the ladders weaving in and out of the trees.

The Gypsies, breakfast fires burning,

haze of wood smoke rising through the trees,
the tantalising waft of bacon frying.

The weight of harvested plums pulling at your waist,
the thick leather belt to support them.
The woven willow basket so cleverly constructed
to withstand the passage of so much fruit,
fleetingly into and then out to box, chip or tray.
The ladder that enables you to reach the
most sun-kissed plums from the top of the tree,
itself constructed from another wood, grown
and used for a different purpose to your own.
Two types of wood, fleetingly merged together
in intimate embrace, lain in the cradle of your branches
for support, to plunder the harvest that you
unfailingly produce each year, frost permitting.

And then on, to the next tree, and on,
returning on an annual basis to renew acquaintances once
more, same tree, same ladder, same branch, same picker.
Brought together once more for a moment in time
of fleeting friendship and intimacy.

You stop for breakfast and in the lull
catch a flash of Woodpecker between the trees.
The Robin, always there, red breasted to greet you,
bright eye alert for the crumbs from your table.
The ever present buzz of striped Wasp busy
plundering the sweet plum juices.
Bright Red Admirals glide down the rows in
search of heady nectar from the fallen fruits.

The trees settle as the pickers move on.
Each one hand pruned by its picker.
Their fruits gone, branches stripped bare,
leaves, twigs, lay strewn on the ground.
Like a minor hurricane has passed.
Odd branches lie snapped and broken, strangely
out of place in the grass between the rows.

Only a few feet from where they formed an
integral part of the green canopy of the Orchard.
The grass lies trampled, by feet, boxes, tractor tyre
marks weaving up the rows around the branches.

And after, the silence descends, peace once more.
The Rabbits creep from the hedgerow to
feed once again on the lush green grass.
The Woodpecker once more traverses the trunks,
raiding its neatly arranged larder, courtesy of man.
All this, repeated, year after year, over such time.
Always slightly different, never the same.

Now just a memory, lost in time, never to be repeated.
Your roots, your life, intermingled with the roots of the
Orchard trees that bring forth such bounty year after year.
How can you replace this closeness with earth, with nature,
the feeling of being part of the landscape, of belonging.
Now the Orchards are gone, trees grubbed out, wildlife
gone, turned to boring fields of chemically fattened grain,
covered with roads or houses. What a loss, what a memory.

Cynthia

From your far African shore,
what made you take flight and soar
on wings adorned, traced with lace,
across the seas our summer to grace.
What brought you here, how did you know
we had flowers to feed you, make you grow.
To sustain you in your hour of need,
satisfy your hunger, after such a deed.

In your millions, a flickering tide,
on warm southerly air currents ride,
soaring over mountains, across Atlantic sea.
So fragile, such a distance, how could it be?
You crowd upon our waiting flowers
sipping nectar through sunlit hours.
Where is it that you make your bed
when moon and stars shine overhead?

As our fields are lit by warm sun's rays,
you rise early, to greet halcyon days.
Searching for blooms to breakfast on,
a short sweet sip, and then you're gone.
On and on, from flower to flower,
enjoy, enjoy each splendid sunlit hour.
Summer lady, painted though you may be,
dressed in all your finery, a picture to see.

No artist if beauty trying to evoke could
have created such loveliness in a stroke.
With your subtle colours and gliding flight
you are such a very welcome sight.
Each year may you deign to visit our shore.
Over flower filled meadows and fields to soar.
Sweet lady, you express summer, freedom of the skies,
Nature, pleasure, in pretty painted disguise.

Walking for Wildlife

All that preparation, sponsor forms, checking the route,
marking it out, organising the children and the parents.
An awful lot of arranging, hard work and dedication,
arriving, unloading, setting up stalls.
The hustle and bustle, chatter of expectant children,
enthusiastic, Walking for Wildlife, tension building.
Send out the marshals to their posts,
lined up, waiting, chaffing at the bit.

They're off, rushing, running, headlong through the bog,
a race to see how fast they can complete the course.
How many miles, how many sponsors, how much money,
racing down the slope, carried away by their own momentum,
to be stopped at the bottom by the bar over the stile.
The stile already muddied by the passing of walkers' boots.
Besides all this, what else did you see?
did you stop, look and listen, to the wildlife all around.

Bredon standing domelike, dominating the Vale,
lit by the rays of the pale Autumn sun.
Cows contentedly grazing the lush green grass stop
and stare as you pass, who is this invading their pasture?
Inquisitive bullocks, lined up, eyes wide, nostrils flaring,
daring each other to go closer, but too frightened, skittish.
The rustle of Pheasants in the undergrowth, everywhere,
sudden rattle and whirr of wings as they explode into the air.

Hips and haws on the hedgerow, bright in the morning sun,
sharp acid sloes hang from the Blackthorn.
rings of tiny mushrooms in the dew wet grass.
A late Tortoiseshell fluttering feebly in the breeze,
the scales long since worn from its wings,
making them transparent against the bright blue sky.
And up in that blue heaven, Buzzards soaring
and mewing to each other overhead.

Into the woods, the Oaks and the Pines,
sunlight filtering through the leaves Autumnal shades.
Tiny tufts of dew bright green Larch needles,
hanging, picked out by the shafts of light.
The twitter of a Tit flock high overhead,
flitting through the tree tops in search of food.
The breeze follows them, whispering through the branches,
tugging at the weakened stems of the leaves, waiting to fall.

Stop, listen, you can hear the acorns falling, dropping,
bouncing off the branches, nature's own harvest, raining down.
Shed from their cups, they litter the ground under the Oaks.
sharing it with the spiny cases of Sweet Chestnut.
The Ivy, clinging to an old Ash is alive, buzzing
with the insects feeding from its late flowers.

A sulphur yellow flash of sculpted wing
in the sunbeams as a Brimstone passes.
Vistas all around as you circle the hill.
Bredon, Malvern distant, picture blue.
The Cotswold ridge fading into the distance,
in the bright, fresh, hazy autumn light.
The fields, shorn to stubble, harvest gathered in.
Stripes of pale green shoots of weak autumn growth.
Curving, rising, dipping, showing the contours of the land.
Shaped by the plough over thousands of years.

All this wildlife surrounds you as you walk on and on,
till you return to the farm, tired, yet somehow refreshed.
Your mind at rest because of this brush with nature,
for nature, this Walking for Wildlife.
And afterwards, collecting all the markers,
the clearing up, the tidying away, the quiet.
Another walk over, another record sum collected,
till we Walk for Wildlife again next year.

Storm

A palette of sepia and ochre,
fields new ploughed, fresh brown earth.
Rain brightened grass verdant,
regiments of winter wheat spearing to heaven.

Black cloud mountains, water pregnant,
spawn wind ragged squalls of rain
scudding across the valley trapped
between cloud base and land.

The brooding hills suck the heavy load
onto the expectant earth below.
Wispy cloud remnants, slide up over
satiated hills, fly to the horizon.

Sun splinters, filtered through cloud breaks,
glitter back from a chopped lake.
Tranquil river transformed to coiling silver
writhing across the land.

Storm loaded torrent rushing to sea,
banks scoured bare,
engulfed into the seething cauldron
of foaming, turbid, soup.

Rooks launch from tree cliffs into gale's teeth.
Tumbling through arced spectrums of light and rain.
Slipstreaming, triumphantly riding the blasts,
masters of their art, mere storms will not ground them.

Stags bellow, steaming the wind,
bone crack of antlers, bodies heaving, straining.
Coats matted, hooves churning,
rusted Bracken thrashed into mud.

Wind reverberates through the wood.
A roaring express train of sound.
Blizzard plucked leaves whirl in turmoil
and cascade, eddying, to the ground.

Leafy boughs, transformed into cruel whips,
lash the passing air into greater frenzy.
An Ash rattles its keys in defiance
trying to bolt the way through the woods.

There is no respite. There is no escape.
Trees skittle as wind rampages on.
Matchsticked branches litter
the sodden drifts of leaves.

Rain dark trunks silvered in wet light.
Shattered rain pearls mist into droplets.
Pale beams grope through tangled
Branches threading a passage to earth.

Grain

Bread, the staple of life that mattered,
grown from the grain, the seed scattered.
Green spears for the light reaching,
the miracle of life, of growth, teaching.
Growing slowly upwards to your prime,
by hot sun blessed in summertime.
If only we could listen through the years,
to what the warm wind whispers in your ears.
Golden fields of corn in the breeze swaying,
the goodness of life in your grain laying.
Slashed, cut in your prime by whirring blades,
never to see life's autumn shades.
Once you held up golden ears to sky,
now felled, strewn on the floor you lie.
Once field blackened, full of stubble smoke,
as if on life itself you would choke.
Now compacted, netted, tightly tied,
no longer free to wave, the wind to ride.
Impaled by forks, carted, stacked high,
threshed by life, chaff, discarded to die.
Blown away by the winds of strife.
Searching for the grain of life
The grain to sustain and nourish,
grain waiting for growth to flourish.
Sow once more the grain, the seeds,
pray for the weather, fight the weeds.
Like life's ambition, heights to attain,
repeat the cycle, over and over, again.
That eternal promise ever keeping.
Nature’s harvest forever reaping.

Jigsaw

Life is like a jigsaw, sometimes hard to make,
which piece to choose, which path to take.
Sometimes, the pieces don't always fit together,
you struggle on whatever the weather.

Till now there's always been that missing piece.
But at long last my search can cease.
You are it. You have arrived.
Completed the picture before my eyes.

Just how did you and I chance to meet.
Now that it's happened the picture's complete.
Just like a puzzle, the jigsaw of life,
the end of my search, the end of my strife.

Just where, oh where, have you been.
Somewhere hidden where I couldn't have seen.
Now that you're here, the last piece to fit,
together our lives closely we'll knit.

You're the piece that holds it all together.
The piece that helps survive the stormy weather.
The piece that makes my worries cease.
The piece that makes me at peace.

Words

Sketching, drawing, singing praises,
painting pictures with coloured phrases.
From within, underground, like a spring,
to the surface they bubble and bring
a torrent, a rushing stream, like a
dream deep riot of colour they teem.
Set free, like a cloud that's burst,
the page showered, in words immersed.
Surrounded by phrases, suddenly found,
a non stop verbal cavalcade of sound.
Vibrant, full of light, rainbow hues,
pour onto paper before you lose.
Suddenly surfaced, brimming to be said,
sorted, sifted, they must be read.
Tumbling from the tongue they've got to be spoken,
thoughts escaped from the head broken.
A breaking wave, an ocean swell,
letters flowing under your spell.
Released from their unconscious cage.
spilling verbal patterns on the page.
Breach the dam, lift the sluice,
see them pour over, let the flood tide loose.

Drowning

in words.

Fisherman

The river flows slowly by. An old man sits
hunched on the bank. His face reflected in the water,
indistinct, the breeze ruffling the surface, hiding the lines.
A wizened figure, mind brimful like the stream,
memories from long ago, things done, achieved.
Others, tantalisingly close, but slipped away. Still dreaming
of the future, old in body, still young in mind.
The rod, held in his gnarled hands, almost as ancient
as he is. Treasured from childhood, itself holding so many
memories, some caught, some lost, strands in the web of time.
The line floats out across the water as if stretching
back over time. Like his life before him, sometimes swept
by the current, carried here and there. Over fast flowing
rapids, dangerous eddies and whirlpools, through
gently flowing streams, to quiet backwaters.
The bait on the hook, temptingly offered, brings memories
of being caught himself on more than one occasion.
The struggle to get free, finally accomplished,
only to be lured to try once again.
When he was young, he had a vision of himself,
sitting by the river. Soaking up the peace of nature
still dreaming of the big one. Still waiting for love, life,
but now having to acknowledge death also.

Leaf

First dawn cracks, the bud breaks.
Nurtured within the leaf wakes,
unfurling into sharp morning air,
drawing virgin breath, unaware.
Mint green, proudly held aloft,
tender to air's touch, dew soft.
First blinding exposure to light,
burn of sun, hot and bright.

Watch and learn as the wind teases,
playing games, with childish breezes.
Through your veins rich sap flowing,
absorbing, producing, to adult growing.
Shade from noon's heat provided.
Growth to maturity safely guided.

Lifeblood, lifeline, severed, unwanted
chemical residues building, skin leathered.
Hanging, dying, freedom awaits,
dreams of flying, storm awakes.
The wind leaves the tree branches,
a single leaf, in its midst, dances to
earth in evening calm, descended.
Finally fallen, a page, ended.

Layered memories piled high
under a growing dark sky.
Sunset frozen, eaten away,
dying, at the end of day.
Skeletal remains exposed
another year's chapter closed.

Reflections of the Vale pass before my eyes.
Sun setting on the water as the evening dies.
These scenes of life from long ago.
History and time passing slow.

About the Author

Born & bred & still living in the Vale of Evesham Bob Woodroofe's poems appear in many poetry magazines & are performed locally. Inspired by the natural world, the landscape & local tradition he attempts to bring the magic of nature & its restorative & healing qualities to a wider audience.

Also available from the

Greenwood Press
38 Birch Avenue
Evesham
Worcs. WR11 1YJ

website http://greenwoodpress.co.uk

email info@greenwoodpress.co.uk

by Bob Woodroofe

A trilogy of poetry collections from
life & nature in the Vale of Evesham

Nature, Reflections & Spirit of the Vale

In search of greenness

Something Stirred

the Poetry Collection

Pick of the crop

Joint poetry collections by
Sue Johnson & Bob Woodroofe

Tales of Trees** & **Journey

Creative Writing books
by Sue Johnson

Writer's Toolkit & Writer's Toolkit 2, 3 & 4

www.ingramcontent.com/pod-product-compliance
Ingram Content Group UK Ltd.
Pitfield, Milton Keynes, MK11 3LW, UK
UKHW041643190726
13854UKWH00006B/2667